# LEAD GUITAR

# BREAKTHROUGH

*Essential Lessons*

## FRETBOARD NAVIGATION, THEORY & TECHNIQUE

# LUKE ZECCHIN

# FRETBOARD MEMORIZATION WORKSHOP

## Getting lost on the guitar neck?
## Finally, fretboard memorization made easy!

If you like this book, you'll love our *Fretboard Memorization Workshop*! This online master class is your shortcut to demystifying the fretboard puzzle. Here you'll be guided step-by-step through the key concepts, techniques, and exercises needed to master your entire fretboard—quickly and easily. These insights have helped thousands of students worldwide, and we're certain they'll help you too!

For more information, head to **LearnYourFretboard.com**.

*This book is dedicated to my beautiful wife Jasmin. Through the seasons you are evergreen.*

Copyright © 2019 Luke Zecchin

ISBN: 978-0-9925507-4-5

Published by **GuitarIQ.com**

Copyedited by Allister Thompson

Proofread by Dan Foster

Illustrated by Jasmin Zecchin

# Contents

# Get Your Free Online Bonus Now!

This book comes complete with free online bonus material. We've compiled a companion website to enhance your reading experience. Extras include audio examples, backing tracks, bonus downloads, and more!

Get your free bonus content at: **www.guitariq.com/lgb-bonus**

# Preface

Welcome, and thank you for choosing *Lead Guitar Breakthrough*.

Although we often teach music in a linear and methodical way, in reality, for many guitar players this doesn't necessarily reflect the way we learn. Our approach is usually far more *circular*. We piece bits of information together as we go, learning different songs, riffs, shapes, and techniques, constantly revisiting things as our skills improve. While there's nothing wrong with this approach, it has the tendency to leave us with isolated bits of seemingly unrelated information. We may know how to play certain things on the guitar but find it hard to understand how all the pieces fit together.

This book is a resource for those eager to improve their lead guitar skills. However, it wasn't written merely to demonstrate popular guitar licks, show you how to play in one particular style, or break down the solos of your favorite players (although it may inadvertently assist in those pursuits). Here we're concerned with the bigger picture. The essential function of this book is to provide a road map for understanding how things are connected on the fretboard. As such, we'll establish a fundamental framework for navigating the entire guitar neck. This will in turn assist you in developing speed and fluidity in your playing, understanding key centers, using chord progressions, building melodic ideas, and more.

Put simply, this is the book I wish I'd read much earlier in my guitar playing journey. While there are no overnight shortcuts to becoming an accomplished musician, working from a solid foundation will significantly help streamline this process. May this information prove as valuable to you as it has been to me.

I sincerely hope this book sparks a breakthrough in your own playing and becomes a catalyst for continued discovery and inspiration.

—Luke Zecchin

# Introduction

Developing a solid understanding of the fundamentals is invaluable for musicians of any skill level. While this book is a resource for guitar players at various stages in their ability, it was primarily written for those wanting more from their lead playing. As I already alluded to, the focus here isn't solely on how to *do* specific things technically. The primary interest is how to *think* about the things we do creatively.

As stated, this book aims to provide a road map for navigating the fretboard. Drawing on this analogy, a map exists to give us context. It shows us where to go and how best to get there. However, it also assists in two other equally important pursuits: *exploration* and *discovery*. This resource presents a concise and easy-to-follow approach to becoming a more complete guitar player. Above all, though, its most valuable contribution will hopefully be to encourage you to think creatively for yourself.

It's always important to remember that while others may be responsible for the teaching, you're ultimately responsible for the learning. Here we're concerned with the essential concepts for a well-rounded approach to lead guitar playing. The way you experiment with and apply that information is up to you. A book of this nature will necessarily include numerous exercises and practical tips. However, you should always place more value on the concepts (and how they can be applied or adapted elsewhere) rather than the specific exercises or techniques themselves.

Additionally, this content may introduce you to techniques that could feel foreign at first. Remember to take regular playing breaks and be conscious of fatigue or excessive tension in the hands, arms, shoulders, and neck. In keeping with this, the set tempos of each exercise in this book serve only as general suggestions. All exercises should be played at a comfortable tempo that facilitates accuracy. Lastly, it's extremely important to work through the information presented here at your own pace. The measure of a lesson's value is never how quickly you learn something but how well you learn it.

# Tips on Technique

Before we begin, it seems appropriate to briefly cover some basics concerning guitar technique. Admittedly, differences in body type, playing style, and personal preference (among other variables) make it difficult to define a one-size-fits-all approach to playing technique. An overly simple yet still fitting definition of good technique is our ability to maximize *tone* while minimizing *tension*. That is, we're endeavoring to play with fluency, clarity, and accuracy in a way that feels comfortable and natural.

Ideally, playing guitar should feel as effortless as possible. Effortlessness, however, requires practice. It's a byproduct of reliable and efficient technique. With this in mind, here are some key things to consider as you work through this book:

- **Choose a Comfortable Playing Position:** The height and angle of your guitar directly impact the effectiveness of your playing technique. Ideally, your guitar neck should be elevated at a comfortable angle and stay at approximately the same height whether you're sitting or standing.

- **Be Mindful of Your Posture:** Slouching and staying relaxed aren't the same thing. It's very difficult to keep the tension out of your neck, shoulders, and back if you have a tendency to sit awkwardly or hunch over while playing.

- **Relax and Remember to Breathe:** Many guitar players find concentration comes at the expense of forgetting to breathe naturally. This leads to unnecessary tightness and isn't conducive to good technique. Seek to maintain relaxed hands, wrists, and forearms at all times.

- **Avoid Unnecessary Wrist Tension:** Your wrists should stay relatively straight in line with your forearms; this is the position in which they're most comfortable. It's increasingly difficult to move your hands and fingers freely if your wrists are bent at unnatural angles.

- **Monitor Your Thumb Position:** Ideally, for general playing your thumb should sit upright, comfortably across from your 1st finger behind the guitar neck. Raising it too high over the top of the guitar neck will affect the mobility and natural curve of your fingers.

- **Use Your Fingertips:** Unless you're holding down multiple strings, avoid using the pads of your fingers on the fretboard. Allow each finger to angle in comfortably (keeping with their natural curve) and target the area around your fingertips for improved accuracy and control.

- **Gauge Your Pressure:** It's often surprising how little pressure is needed to sound a note cleanly. Remember, there's only a small distance between the bottom of a string and the top of a fret. Avoiding excess pressure will increase speed and agility.

- **Minimize Your Movements:** There's no benefit in unnecessary effort. Keeping fingers close to the fretboard and reducing picking action avoids exaggerating the movement required by either hand. Economizing your technique will help improve speed and consistency.

- **Focus on Efficient Picking:** There'll be less resistance in your picking technique if the guitar pick is positioned at a slight but consistent angle to the strings (not flat or parallel). Play using only the tip of the pick, holding it securely but not tightly for smooth and controlled picking strokes.

- **Listen to Your Body:** Your body will tell you if it's tense or uncomfortable. Listen to it. If playing guitar is painful, you're likely not doing it right. Use any warning signs as an opportunity to reassess the effectiveness of your playing technique. Obviously, seek professional medical advice if required.

1

# Major Building Blocks

*In this first chapter, we take an in-depth look at the major scale and its importance in lead guitar playing.*

# Introduction

In this first section, we'll start by getting our basic musical bearings. This information will be foundational not only to everything covered in this book but also to our general musical understanding. When endeavoring to understand the bigger picture, we must begin with a solid reference point on which to build our overarching framework. In light of this, it's difficult to think of a better starting point for guitar players than the major scale. Chords, pentatonic scales, modes, and arpeggios, for example, are all contained within the major scale. Even musical information that moves outside the major scale structure is still defined by the way it differs from this scale. Simply put, the major scale is a vital part of the fabric holding music together. As such, it should be our first stop when seeking to make sense of the guitar fretboard.

# Our Reference Point

First, let's establish what a major scale looks and sounds like on guitar. Here we have a basic single-octave major scale in the key of G. This scale shape is likely already familiar to a lot of guitar players. Even those who don't know this shape should still find the sound easily recognizable:

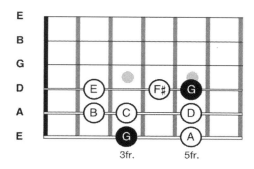

## Exercise 1.1

Note: We'll use G major for the purpose of illustration, but these same patterns and shapes can be shifted up or down to be played in any key.

In order for us to make practical use of this information, let's take a closer look at how a major scale is built. If, for example, we take this same G major scale and lay the notes out horizontally across the low E string, we discover two important things:

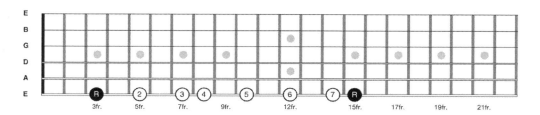

- First, the guitar is an instrument that allows us to play the same thing in multiple ways. This is certainly a recurring theme when learning guitar, and it hints at how we might begin to use the fretboard more comprehensively in our playing. Specific chords and scales aren't limited to one particular shape or position on the guitar neck; rather, they can be expressed in various forms across the fretboard.

- Second, if we attribute a number to each note of the scale, ascending from the root note as demonstrated, we see the essential structure common to all major scales. A major scale is basically a series of whole-step (two-fret) movements. The only exceptions to this are after the $3^{rd}$ and $7^{th}$ notes of the scale. These both ascend by a single half step (one fret). This is the foundational formula that's found in all major scales, regardless of their key or starting position. Just knowing this one simple principle immediately gives us the ability to build a major scale from any note, on any string, across the whole fretboard!

*Tip: Picturing the major scale is like visualizing an eight-step ladder. The third and seventh steps are just half the distance closer than all the others.*

Why is this important for improving our playing? As already highlighted, chords and scales can be played in many different ways across the guitar neck. What becomes essential is developing a system or structure that provides a foundation for visualizing, sorting through, and understanding all the musical information available to us. Since the major scale is central to everything in Western music, it makes sense that this would be the core framework we'd reference on the fretboard.

In other words, once we understand how the major scale is built, we can see that there's an inherent structure or pattern running across the entire fretboard. This is true in all keys, regardless of string or neck position. This structure provides the road map for navigating the fretboard, irrespective of what we're playing or the key we're playing in.

*Tip: Even though looking at the fretboard can initially seem overwhelming, remember that we're only dealing with 12 notes. These notes repeat themselves in a consistent and predictable fashion across the guitar neck. Keeping this in mind will make the fretboard seem significantly more manageable.*

# Our Starting Point

Although it may not yet seem like much, the basic structure we've just looked at is foundational to all popular music. We've established that in any key there's a consistent pattern across all strings. The task now becomes finding the best way to organize this information into more easily understandable sections. This process will become clearer in the next chapter.

Before delving into how all the pieces fit together, let's begin by checking out the first scale pattern we'll use as our starting point:

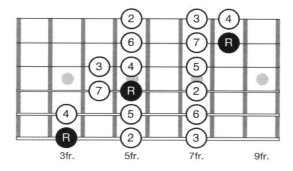

## Exercise 1.2

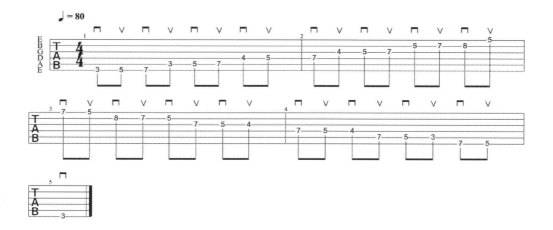

You can see that we're using the same major scale as before, but here it's being played in a different way. We're now spanning this scale across multiple octaves and are playing it in a way that places three notes on each string. This hints at the two real benefits to this approach:

- First, spanning a shape over multiple octaves maximizes the reach of that pattern within a single playing position. Put simply, we have more fretboard real estate available to us within a single area.

- Second, using three notes per string allows us to easily incorporate a wider range of techniques (such as economy picking or legato) into our playing. As we'll see in later chapters, this becomes an intuitive way of structuring melodic ideas for those who want to develop more speed and fluidity in their playing.

Note: Additionally, this scale shape highlights the three basic patterns our fingers will encounter when playing three notes per string in this way. They're as follows:

- Three notes separated by a whole step each (W/W).

- Three notes separated by a half step and then a whole step (H/W).

- Three notes separated by a whole step and then a half step (W/H).

For this scale and subsequent scales in this book, the suggested left-hand fingerings are:

- Using the 1st, 2nd, and 4th fingers for both W/W and H/W movements.

- Using the 1st, 3rd, and 4th fingers for W/H movements.

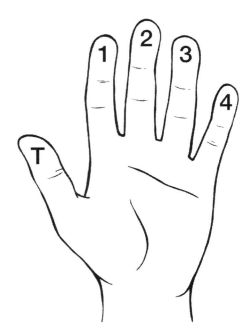

**Tip:** *Built from the G note on the 3rd fret of the low E string, this scale pattern represents G major. If we built this shape from the F note on the 1st fret of the same string, our key center would logically change to F major. As such, learning to refer to notes by their respective numbers (often called degrees) will be of great benefit. Each number references a note's distance from the root note, or rather, its interval relationship to the root note. Although scale notes will change depending on the key we're playing in, the scale pattern will stay the same. In other words, in moving this shape around the guitar neck, the intervals stay the same regardless of the notes they represent.*

# Warming Up

For guitarists new to lead playing or who are mainly used to pentatonic scales, playing three notes per string can seem difficult at first. Below is a basic exercise to help familiarize our fingers with this new way of playing.

Note: It's important to use specific finger positions to maximize the effectiveness of this exercise. The initial line below should be played using the 1st and 2nd fingers. The middle line should be played using the 2nd and 4th fingers. And the last line should be played using the 1st and 4th fingers.

## Exercise 1.3

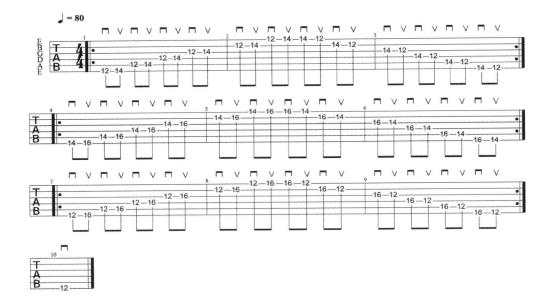

*Tip: Once this feels comfortable and fluent, work on moving this exercise down toward the 1st fret. Focus on doing this one fret at a time to help your fingers adjust to the wider spacing at lower frets.*

# Focus Points

- Become familiar with the basic formula of how a major scale is built. Understand that in any given key this formula simply repeats across each string horizontally, just from different starting points in the scale.

- Focus on the outlined major scale shape (using three notes per string) until playing it feels controlled and natural. Experiment with shifting this scale shape around the guitar neck in different keys.

- Make use of the warm-up exercise provided as a way to build greater strength and dexterity in the left hand.

2

# Seven Essential Shapes

*Having centered our focus on the major scale, now we'll discuss its wider implications for fretboard navigation.*

# Introduction

In the previous chapter, we discussed how the major scale is central to almost everything else in music. We established that understanding the way this scale is built gives us a road map for navigating through any key across the entire fretboard. This provides a foundational reference point for understanding and communicating our musical ideas in any position on the guitar neck. In this chapter, we further unpack this concept, demonstrating how to view this information practically on the fretboard and providing the tools to begin piecing everything together.

# Laying the Foundations

As previously stated, the major scale provides an inherent structure that runs across the entire guitar neck. Below are two diagrams demonstrating what the notes of a major scale look like when mapped across the complete fretboard. These examples again use the G major scale. As already established, this pattern is the same in any key, because the major scale structure doesn't change. For example, if we wanted to play in the key of A, this entire pattern would just shift up a whole step. The highlighted root notes would then align with A, not G:

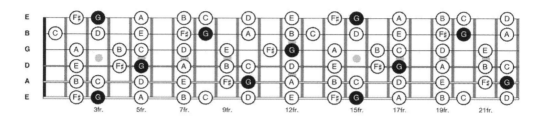

This second diagram mirrors the first but alternatively represents each note by its relative number. You can see that the ascending pattern is consistent on all strings. Each individual string just starts from a different point in the scale:

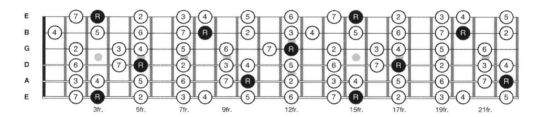

Admittedly, when we map out notes like this, it can look fairly complex at first. As we'll see, the real trick is to visualize the various parts that make up the whole. This involves isolating the smaller scale shapes found within this larger framework.

> *Tip: Remember, because the notes on a guitar repeat from the 12th fret, the bottom half of the guitar neck is the same as the top half. This means that any pattern across the fretboard is only half as complicated as it first appears.*

# The Modal Framework

It's helpful at this point to introduce a brief discussion on the *modes* of the major scale. You may have heard this term before. What exactly are the modes, and how are they relevant? Even though there seems to be a little confusion surrounding the topic of modes, the basic concept is relatively simple. Essentially, modes can be understood as inversions or alternate voicings of the major scale. In other words, modes use the same notes as the major scale they relate to, but they're built from different starting points within that scale. This will become clearer as we move through this chapter.

Understood fully, the modes of the major scale can function as unique scales within their own right. Each mode has its own unique flavor or tonal characteristic that sets it apart from the others. A more advanced application of the modes opens some interesting and creative possibilities for songwriting and improvisation. This is precisely why they're so popular among many guitar players.

Even without an in-depth understanding of modal theory, however, this concept is still very useful. This book is concerned with laying solid foundations on which to build our understanding. In the context of fretboard navigation, each mode can function as an alternate position of the major scale as we move around the guitar neck.

Thus far, we've seen how a major scale is built and what it looks like when mapped across the entire fretboard. If the task is to divide this information into smaller, more digestible sections, it's hard to think of a better system than the modal framework. To do this, visualize once again the notes of a major scale laid out horizontally across the low E string (demonstrated in **Chapter 1**). We'll now start building alternate positions of this scale, starting from each degree.

Note: For a more in-depth discussion on understanding and using modes, please refer to my book ***Learn Your Guitar Scales***.

# Shape 1

The good news is you already know the 1st position:

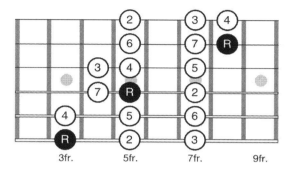

As we've seen, this is the 1st position of the major scale. Alternatively, you may have traditionally heard it referred to as the *Ionian* mode.

## Exercise 2.1

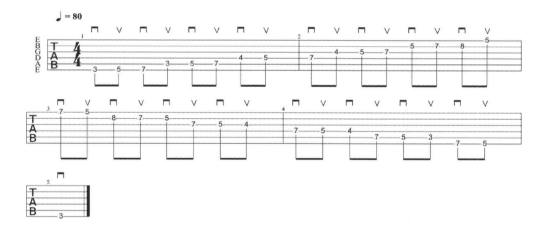

Note: When demonstrating a scale, it's common to extend it from one root note to another. Since the purpose here is to cover as much ground as possible, we're adding more notes from the scale on the high E string. While it's useful to visualize all three extra notes, only two of them will be used in these exercises.

# Shape 2

Now let's take a look at the next scale position, starting from the 5th fret:

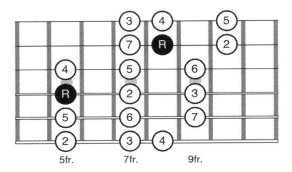

Here we have the 2nd position of the G major scale. Built from the 2nd degree, traditionally this scale could also be referred to as the *Dorian* mode.

## Exercise 2.2

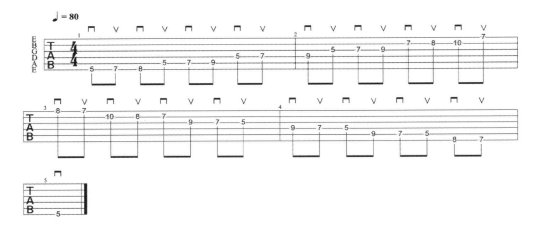

Note: Correctly represented in its modal context, this would be the A Dorian scale, meaning A would be represented as the root note or 1st degree. This would subsequently change the interval relationship (or numbers) for the rest of the notes, even though the pattern itself wouldn't change. However, because we're primarily treating these shapes as alternate positions of G major, we'll continue referencing G as our root note throughout these examples.

# Shape 3

Here we have the next position, starting at the 7$^{th}$ fret:

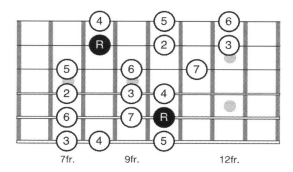

This is the 3$^{rd}$ position of the G major scale. Built from the 3$^{rd}$ degree, this scale could also be referred to as the *Phrygian* mode.

## Exercise 2.3

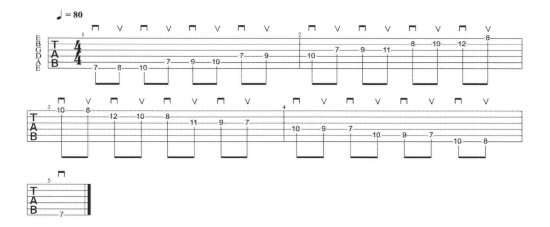

# Shape 4

This is the next shape, starting at the 8th fret:

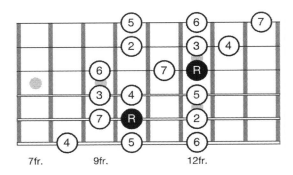

7fr.        9fr.        12fr.

Here we have the 4th position of the G major scale. This scale is built from the 4th degree and is commonly referred to as the *Lydian* mode.

## Exercise 2.4

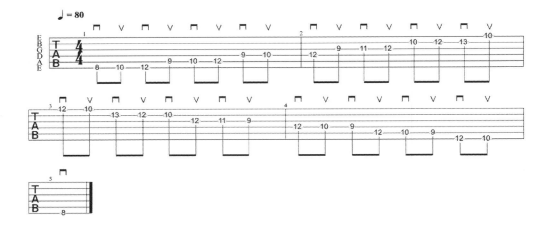

# Shape 5

The next pattern starts from the 10<sup>th</sup> fret:

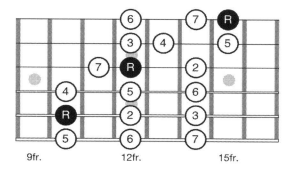

9fr.        12fr.        15fr.

This is the 5<sup>th</sup> position of G major. It's built from the 5<sup>th</sup> degree of the scale and is also referred to as the *Mixolydian* mode.

## Exercise 2.5

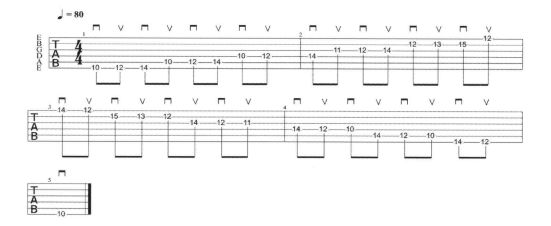

# Shape 6

Here's the next position, starting at the 12th fret:

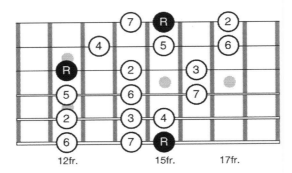

12fr.        15fr.        17fr.

This is the 6th position of G major. We build this scale from the 6th degree, and it's also known as the *Aeolian* mode.

## Exercise 2.6

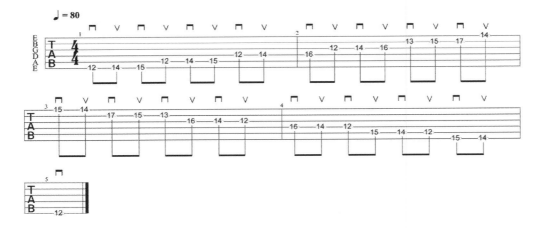

Note: This scale is also commonly referred to as the *natural minor* scale. Although we're using the notes of G major, when we start at the 6th degree we actually build an E minor scale. This hints at the way modes function. They shift the tonal center of one scale and in doing so create another scale.

*Tip: As we'll see, each pattern functions in the context of both major and minor keys. This means these major scale patterns aren't limited to use over major progressions when we're songwriting or improvising.*

# Shape 7

Lastly, we have the next position, starting from the 14th fret:

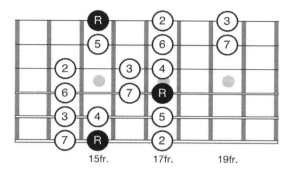

This is the 7th and final position of G major. We build this scale from the 7th degree, and it's alternatively known as the *Locrian* mode.

# Exercise 2.7

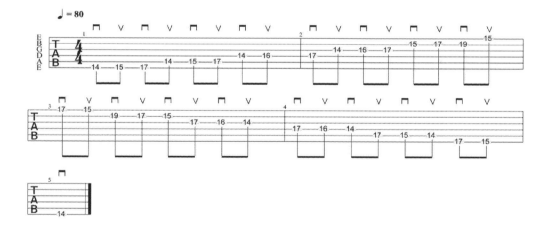

# Putting It All Together

Compare each shape in the previous sections with the full-scale diagrams at the beginning of this chapter. What do you notice? The entire guitar neck has been covered by these seven shapes, repeating in sequence. Don't underestimate how valuable this information will become. We aren't learning scales for the purpose of just *learning scales*! We learn them because they provide an essential blueprint for playing over any key, in any position on the fretboard. Therefore, it's important to focus on memorizing each shape separately before moving on to the next position.

Once comfortable playing each position, it's helpful to practice moving through each pattern in sequence. You can do this simply by playing through one position several times before ascending to the next position and repeating the process.

Note: Remember to make use of the recommended fingerings in **Chapter 1** for each scale shape. Basic alternate down/up picking strokes have been suggested for these exercises. However, as we'll see, once you become more comfortable with these patterns, you'll find they accommodate a broad range of techniques.

*Tip: It's beneficial to practice visualizing the location of the root notes in each scale position. This provides a reference point on the guitar neck. For example, say you wanted to play a melodic idea on a particular part of the fretboard. It's more intuitive knowing the scale position attached to the root notes in that area than counting from the 1st position to find the right shape.*

# The Bigger Picture

Our starting point has been to visualize the isolated scale positions found across the guitar neck. However, if our goal is to freely navigate the entire fretboard, we'll want to begin visualizing the neck as a whole. We need to view all these pieces as *connected* in order to move effortlessly through each position when playing. In fact, given a little time, it's possible to view the entire fretboard as one extended scale when playing in any key.

Below we have another diagram using the notes of G major. Here it's narrowed down to start at the 1st position (3rd fret) and end at this same position an octave higher (15th fret). Whereas before this might have seemed like a random cross-section of notes, now we can discern the internal structure of this pattern. We do this by pinpointing each of the seven shapes we've learned within the larger framework. Once we can locate each shape, we're able to observe how these patterns are connected. Each position simply begins in between the overlapping patterns on either side:

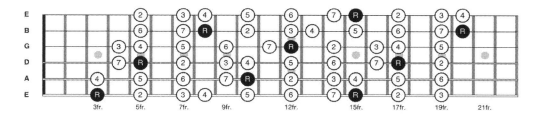

*Tip: Again, it's extremely useful to view the root notes as anchor points within each scale pattern. Locating root notes isn't just about finding our way around; it's also important for structuring melodic ideas. This is especially true when using additional shapes like pentatonic scales or arpeggios within this framework or attempting to play over key changes.*

# Ascending & Descending

Now it's time to put our hard work to the test! Here are two fantastic exercises for connecting each section of the larger framework we've been working with. These exercises will assess our success in familiarizing ourselves with each individual position. Here we'll ascend and descend alternately through each pattern until we've come full circle around the guitar neck. Admittedly, this can be difficult at first. Initially, it may be easier to cycle through just two or three shapes at a time until you're able to play these entire exercises in full.

Note: Although each exercise can be played using alternate picking, for maximum speed and fluidity, experiment with the outlined picking technique. These exercises demonstrate a popular *economy* approach to playing three-note-per-string patterns. Here we use consecutive downstrokes when ascending from one string to another and consecutive upstrokes when descending the alternate way.

The first part of this exercise ascends from the 1<sup>st</sup> position.

## Exercise 2.8

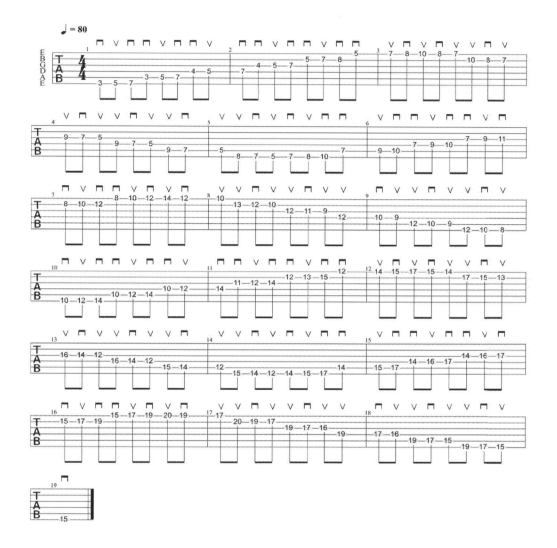

The second part of this exercise descends from the 1$^{st}$ position, one octave higher.

# Exercise 2.9

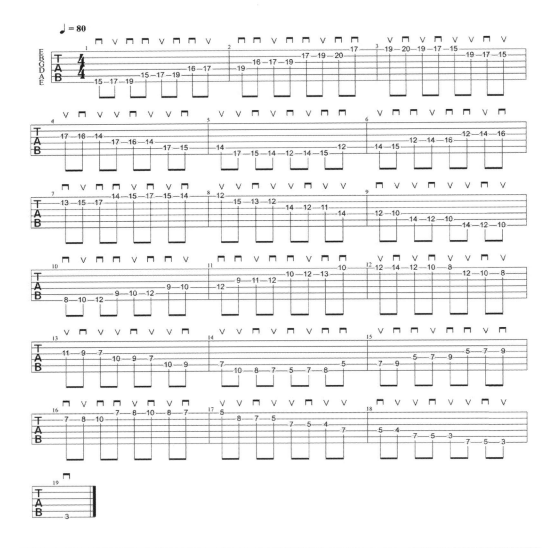

# Focus Points

- Learn each of the outlined scale patterns in full. They'll become fundamental for moving forward in this book (and in your wider guitar pursuits). Again, concentrate on each shape separately before moving on to the next position.

- Practice visualizing how each individual pattern overlaps and interconnects with the surrounding shapes. And become familiar with locating the root notes within each scale position.

- Focus on practicing the **Ascending & Descending** exercises outlined. Remember to start slowly and be as accurate as possible, breaking down these exercises to focus initially on smaller sections if necessary.

3

# Creative Navigation

*Now that we have a solid framework in place, this chapter looks at techniques for working more creatively with these patterns on the fretboard.*

# Introduction

So far, we've highlighted how the major scale exists as a foundational structure across the entire fretboard. We then discussed isolating and learning the particular positions that make up this larger framework. The task now is making this information more useable in real musical applications. As helpful as scales are, the end goal is always to do something creative and musical with what we've learned. One way to practice this is by introducing more interesting ways of playing these patterns using various scale *sequences*.

In the first chapter, we mentioned that three-note-per-string patterns are compatible with a wide range of playing techniques. Having already introduced the concept of economy picking (in **Chapter 2**), we'll now demonstrate some other popular approaches to experiment with.

Note: For simplicity, all examples will be demonstrated using the 1$^{st}$ position of G major. The main thing isn't the scale shape, but rather the *sequence* being applied to the shape. Each technique will translate to any position we've looked at. You may find it more comfortable to practice these sequences higher on the fretboard. Additionally, the suggested tempo for these exercises is 100 BPM. This is only a guide; it's important to start by practicing each exercise accurately at a comfortable tempo.

# Sequence 1 | Alternate Picking (A)

This initial sequence doubles as an exercise in alternate picking. The sequence moves three steps forward, one step back through the scale. Used in small bursts, this concept is a popular way to create more mileage when ascending or descending through smaller note groupings within a scale pattern.

## Exercise 3.1

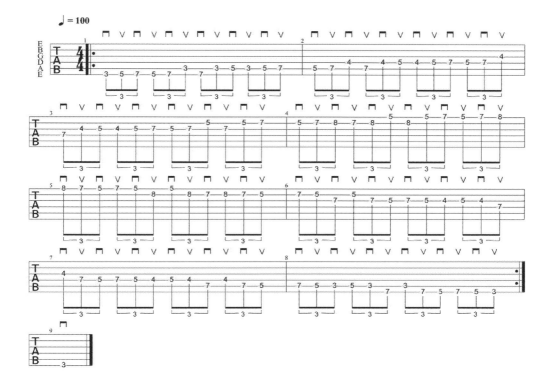

*Tip:* Building speed in our playing is first and foremost a byproduct of accuracy. One key to playing fast is actually learning to play slowly. Make sure you achieve accuracy and consistency in your technique at slower tempos before trying to increase your speed.

# Sequence 2 | Alternate Picking (B)

In this next sequence, we're again practicing our alternate picking. Here we're simply adding repetition to the scale as we move through each string. This is a common technique for extending scale runs and building up picking speed.

## Exercise 3.2

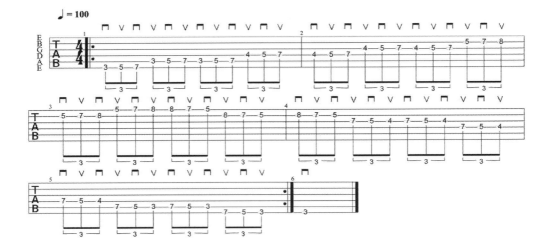

Tip: Many guitarists find smaller, thicker, and sharper guitar picks more conducive to faster playing. Experiment with holding the pick at a 45-degree angle to the strings to help minimize unnecessary movements in your picking action.

# Sequence 3 | Legato (A)

In this sequence, we're applying a series of hammer-ons and pull-offs (often referred to as *legato*) to ascend and descend through the scale. Similar to the first exercise in this chapter, we're again moving three steps forward, one step back through the scale. This time, however, each step represents a string instead of a single note. This is a popular technique for building strength and speed in our left hand.

## Exercise 3.3

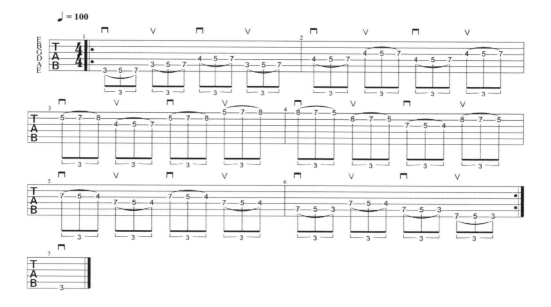

*Tip: Here we're only picking the first note of each beat. We're then using our left hand to hammer-on or pull-off the notes following on each string (depending on whether the sequence is ascending or descending). Be sure to keep each note consistent in volume with the initial picked note, letting each one ring clearly for its full duration.*

# Sequence 4 | Legato (B)

This next pattern again uses a popular legato sequence for developing strength and fluidity in the left hand. In contrast to the previous exercise, this sequence starts with a pull-off. It then moves through a simple repetitive cycle that's looped on each string as we move through the scale.

## Exercise 3.4

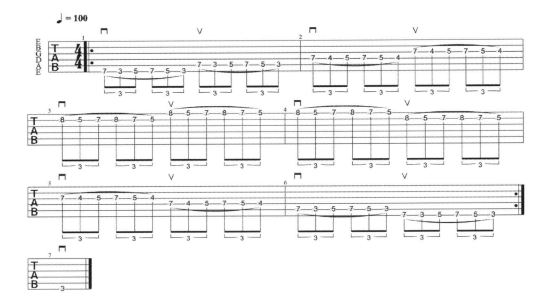

*Tip:* In addition to consistency in volume, be sure to focus on consistency in timing. Legato should ideally sound like a fluid movement between notes. Developing a smooth, flowing motion in your playing involves cultivating a keen awareness for both dynamics and timing.

# Sequence 5 | String Skipping

Next we have a string-skipping sequence, again using this legato technique. Here we're moving through the pattern by missing a string and then doubling back. In addition to mixing up the way we usually play through scales, this sequence will test and train the accuracy of our left hand.

## Exercise 3.5

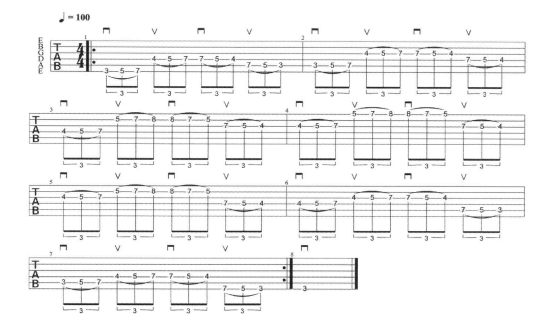

> *Tip:* *Accuracy involves playing the correct notes cleanly with clear sustain and no unnecessary string noise. Concentrate on fretting notes with precision, using the tips of your fingers. Avoid lazy, clumsy, or unintentional contact between the strings and your left hand.*

# Sequence 6 | Odd Note Groupings

This final sequence is an example of how unusual note groupings can add interest to our phrasing. We often think in terms of *even* phrases that consistently land on the same beat. Instead, here we're grouping sections in five-note repetitions using legato as we move through the scale. This technique is a creative way to mix up the more typical melodic groupings we're used to hearing.

## Exercise 3.6

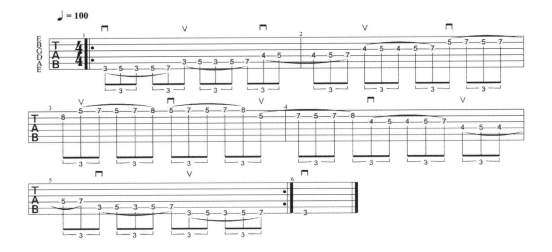

*Tip: Speed isn't just about playing things faster. A great way to experiment with different speeds is by changing the rhythm, not the tempo. Each exercise outlined in this chapter uses triplets (three notes per beat). However, these sequences could also be played using $8^{th}$ notes (two notes per beat), $16^{th}$ notes (four notes per beat), or even $16^{th}$ note triplets (six notes per beat). Try experimenting with the way simple changes in rhythm can completely alter the sound and speed of a pattern.*

# A Quick Note on Speed

Unfortunately, developing speed is sometimes emphasized over other aspects of guitar playing that are equally, if not more, important. Consider the importance of a great ear for melody, having solid rhythm, thinking creatively, and being sensitive to feel, dynamics, and emotion in a song. These things will get you much further as a musician than just being able to play something *fast*.

However, since so many guitarists still seem fascinated with speed, there are some essentials to keep in mind. Building speed in your playing is a byproduct of two key things:

- **Accuracy:** As already stated, one key to playing fast is first learning to play slowly. It's important to remember that playing something *fast* isn't the same as playing something *badly at a fast tempo*. Make sure you achieve accuracy and consistency in your technique at slower tempos before trying to increase your speed.

- **Economy:** Ever wondered why fast playing often looks effortless? That's because it often is! Economy is about not expending any more effort than is actually required. Smooth, relaxed movements are far more conducive to faster playing than tense, rigid movements. In addition to keeping as relaxed as possible, we want to focus on minimizing the movements our hands are making (in terms of their distance from the strings). Perhaps it's more helpful to think about speed as the result of smaller, more efficient movements as opposed to just *quicker* ones.

# Get Creative

For those wanting to push themselves further, why not combine each sequence in this chapter with the **Ascending & Descending** exercises covered in the previous chapter? Try applying each specific sequence to both exercises. You could even experiment with playing randomly through different sequences each time you ascend or descend an alternate position.

Ultimately, the sequences covered in this chapter represent just a handful of ideas for navigating scale positions more creatively. As always, these are just suggestions to help you think for yourself. Practice mixing up techniques (e.g., using legato on picked sequences and picking on legato sequences), or better yet, come up with new sequences and patterns of your own.

It's important to remember that in real musical situations, we'd hopefully do something more dynamic than just playing scale sequences. However, used in small bursts, sequence ideas can be very handy for moving between different parts of the fretboard. They're also useful for connecting melodic lines and adding flourishes of speed or intensity to your playing. So let your ears guide you and keep experimenting!

# Focus Points

- Using the 1$^{st}$ position of the major scale, practice the sequences outlined in this chapter at a slow tempo. Experiment with these sequences in different keys. (They may initially feel more comfortable played higher on the guitar neck.) Try increasing the tempo or moving to faster rhythms when each sequence can be played fluently.

- Once these sequences feel comfortable using the 1$^{st}$ position, try applying them to alternate positions of the major scale. Remember, because each pattern uses three notes per string, all sequences are easily transferable between scale positions.

- Try mixing up sequences with the various techniques demonstrated in this chapter (alternate picking, legato, etc.). Experiment with different rhythms and try to come up with some sequences of your own. Explore how you might use small bursts of these sequence ideas *musically* in your playing.

4

# Breaking Boundaries

*This chapter discusses techniques for moving outside scale positions and finding new ways to experiment with melodic ideas on the fretboard.*

# Introduction

In the previous chapters, we became familiar with some fundamental shapes. We established that these patterns provide a framework for successfully finding our way around the fretboard (regardless of the key center). And we experimented with various ways to apply this information more creatively. This alone offers a huge contribution to any guitarist seeking a more extensive understanding of the fretboard. Visualizing these alternate positions of the major scale across the entire fretboard provides a comprehensive map for crafting musical ideas in any position.

Having laid the groundwork, it now becomes important to *break out* of these core patterns that we've learned. This doesn't negate the importance of these shapes in establishing our fundamental framework. Instead, it's a means of further enhancing and exploring the ways we can creatively apply this information.

# Let's Get Horizontal

*Vertical* scale shapes (like the ones we've been working with) make sense for maximizing our reach within a small area on the fretboard. However, they also limit us to playing within a single position. One of the easiest ways to break out of common scale forms is to visualize them *horizontally* across the guitar neck.

Being able to play through scale patterns in this way is immensely beneficial. It assists in navigating alternate positions with ease and opens up new ways of reinterpreting familiar patterns and ideas. Additionally, this approach allows us to cover a lot of ground quickly when playing.

**Tip:** *This isn't as complicated as it initially seems. Remember, we already know the formula of a major scale. It's a series of whole steps, except for the half-step movements after the 3rd and 7th notes. Each string just starts from a different point in this sequence (e.g., in the 1st position, the 5th string starts at the 4th degree, and so on). Therefore, on any string, this formula tells us where we are in relation to the next note. In other words, each scale number indicates whether the next note is a whole step or half step away.*

# Single-String Exercises

Below is an example of how to practice this idea by isolating one string at a time. In this exercise, we start on the high E string and ascend three notes at a time. Playing 8th notes, we'll move from the 1st position to the octave higher and then back down again.

Remember, each string repeats the simple major scale structure we're already familiar with. Here it's just starting from the 2nd degree of the scale:

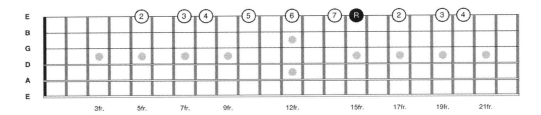

## Exercise 4.1

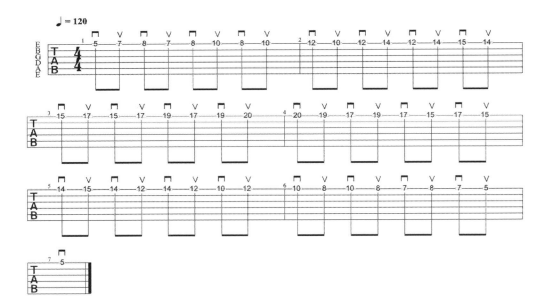

Note: Experiment with this exercise across all six strings. Focus on one string at a time, counting up and back through the scale degrees before moving on to the next string. When you're comfortable with this, try looping through each individual string in order, starting from the 6th string.

# Double-String Exercises

Another useful approach for navigating the fretboard horizontally is to practice using multiple sets of strings. In this exercise, we'll ascend and descend in triplets, moving back and forth through each position horizontally, using only the B and E strings.

As you can see, in this example we're focusing on just the 1st and 2nd strings, starting at the 1st position and looping through each subsequent shape:

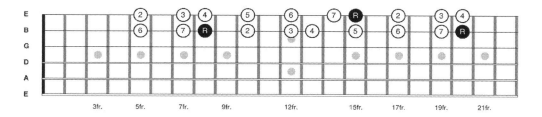

## Exercise 4.2

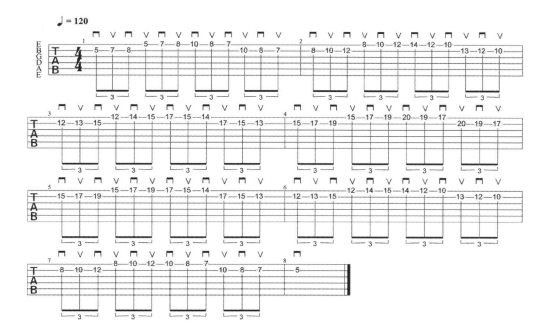

Note: Experiment with shifting this exercise to each set of adjacent strings. Focus on two strings at a time, counting through each scale position as you go. When this feels comfortable, try looping through each set of strings in order, starting from the 5th and 6th strings.

# Scales Within Scales

Let's continue this horizontal exploration across the fretboard. In **Chapter 1**, we established that the same idea can be played in multiple ways on the guitar neck. There isn't one particular way to play a certain scale. In fact, because each of the seven positions we've looked at spans multiple octaves, it's possible to isolate numerous single-octave scales within each position. For example, condensing the 1st position of G major to a single octave gives us a smaller shape that repeats throughout the larger framework. The only difference with these shapes is that notes on the first two strings are raised by a half step (because of the guitar's tuning):

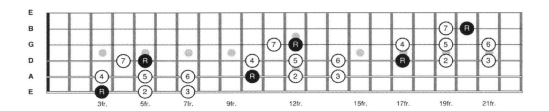

Notice that these aren't really *new* shapes; they're just found within the larger patterns we already know. Having looked at navigating scale positions horizontally using one or two strings, we'll now look at isolating these single-octave shapes across three strings. In this exercise, we'll play back and forth through each single-octave shape on the G, B, and E strings, using 16th notes.

# Exercise 4.3

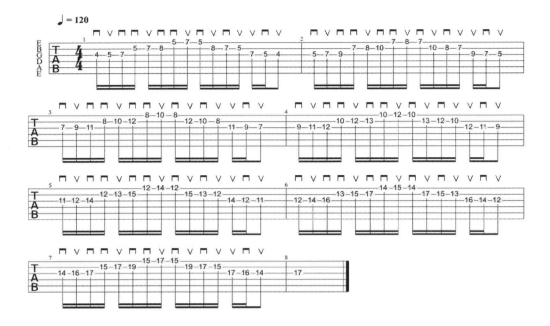

**Tip:** *Again, try not to look at these as new shapes. We're just isolating smaller positions within the larger framework we've already learned. Focus on the way each position of the major scale can be viewed as a single-octave shape that repeats various times throughout the larger scale shapes.*

Note: Experiment with this exercise using single-octave shapes, starting from the 4th, 5th, and 6th strings. Once this feels natural, play through each single-octave shape in order, starting from the 6th string.

# Let's Get Diagonal

Lastly, having explored various approaches to navigating major scale positions horizontally when playing, we can still push this *scales within scales* concept a little further. The example below isolates a single octave of the major scale on the 5th and 6th strings. This basic double-string shape enables us to do something quite interesting. As we'll see, this exact pattern repeats itself diagonally across the fretboard in numerous octaves. Being able to visualize a pattern in this way allows us to shift through various positions, covering an enormous amount of ground quite quickly. This type of diagonal repetition is a popular approach for stringing together blitzing runs up or down the guitar neck:

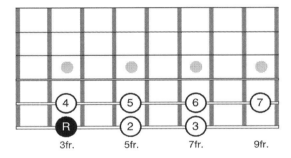

Let's see what this might look like using the 1st position. In this example, we'll use legato to play through each shape repetition in groups of 16th note triplets.

## Exercise 4.4

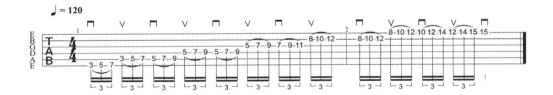

Another popular way to apply this concept is to simplify the scale shape down to just six notes, as demonstrated. In leaving out the 7th note of a pattern, we're left with an even easier shape to repeat across the various octaves. The example shown here uses the 7th position:

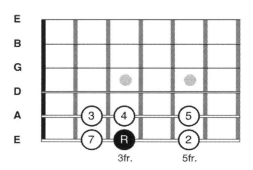

## Exercise 4.5

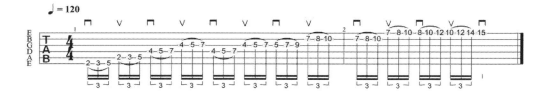

Note: Experiment with both diagonal approaches from each scale position along the 6th string. Try applying various sequences of your own to these repetitive diagonal patterns and explore using the different playing techniques we've covered previously.

# Visualization Recap

In this chapter, we've covered four different visualization methods. These help us navigate or break out of the shapes that establish our larger framework. They enhance our ability to use this central framework creatively in a wide range of musical applications. To briefly recap, these methods have focused on:

- **Scale Degrees:** Moving through the scale *degrees* horizontally on each individual string.

- **Scale Positions:** Navigating through the scale *positions* horizontally by limiting ourselves to just two strings.

- **Octave Shapes:** Isolating the single-octave scale *shapes* within the larger framework by moving around the guitar neck across three strings.

- **Diagonal Repetitions:** Pinpointing the various scale *repetitions* that occur when navigating the fretboard in a more diagonal fashion.

A familiarity with multiple ways of interpreting the bigger picture into its smaller components is key for mastering the fretboard. The ability to focus on particular sections of the guitar neck while maintaining an awareness of how each section is connected is a *big* step toward thinking like a pro. Ultimately, you're working toward viewing all this information simultaneously. This will enable you to navigate creatively through different methods and techniques in a way that sounds uninhibited and musical.

*Tip: Often, limiting ourselves to particular strings or sections of the fretboard can be helpful creatively. This is because we force ourselves to look at things from a different perspective. Always experiment with playing the same thing in different ways. Not only will this consolidate your knowledge of the fretboard, but you also just might discover something new in the process!*

# Focus Points

- Work on the exercises in this chapter. Remember, speed isn't the goal just yet. Play at tempos you find comfortable and ensure you aren't making mistakes in attempting to rush through each exercise.

- Practice applying the concepts outlined in this chapter to alternate strings and positions on the guitar. Try to view each note being played in the context of the larger framework. Understand that these horizontal and diagonal patterns aren't *new* sequences to learn; they're just different ways of viewing the patterns we already know.

- Think about the various visualization methods highlighted in each exercise. Experiment with how you might use these alternate ways of visualizing scale patterns creatively in your own playing.

5

# Constructing Chords

*Now let's shift focus slightly and look at some foundational concepts in music theory relating to the framework we've established.*

# Introduction

Until now, the bulk of information covered in this book has been tailored largely to the practical. That is, our introduction to the modes has explored what they look like in various shapes and forms, how this framework is foundational to fretboard navigation, and how we can start working creatively with this information. Now that we've established a comprehensive fretboard map, the task is to build our understanding around this central framework.

Understanding the major scale and its various positions provides an extensive structure for navigating the guitar neck in any key. However, as we'll see, this framework also has a wider *theoretical* application. This structure enables us to understand how chords are built and how chord progressions relate to certain keys. It's difficult to fully appreciate how to craft melodic ideas in a song without some understanding of the way chords work. As such, a basic understanding of chord theory is fundamental for both rhythm and lead playing alike.

# Stacking Intervals

When we talk about playing in a particular major key (or playing *diatonically*), we mean that notes used to construct chords and melodies come from the same major scale. There's actually a wide range of sonic diversity in the chords we can construct, starting from the different degrees of a major scale. This is done by stacking multiple intervals on top of one another, using the major scale positions as our reference. The simplest form of these chords is built from stacking notes on top of each other in groups of three. This is how basic major, minor, and diminished chords (also known as *triads*) are created.

This process uses the 1st note of a scale position as the chord's starting root note. Since notes too close to one another often sound tense or dissonant when played together, these are avoided in basic chords. This means only notes greater than a whole step apart are used in standard triads. In other words, we pick our starting root note, leapfrog the 2nd note in the scale, stack the 3rd note on the root, skip the 4th, and then stack the 5th on top.

Looking at a single octave of the 1st position (the Ionian mode), this leaves us with the three notes of a major chord. If we play these notes together, reordering them to make things easy on our fingers, we get the familiar E barre chord shape. From the 3rd fret, this gives us a G chord:

I

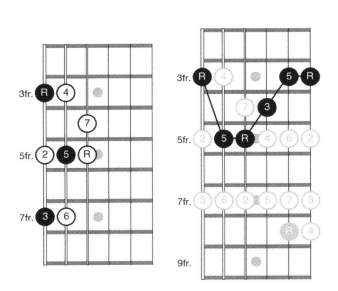

Now we can repeat this process to find the second chord of a major scale, built from the 2nd degree:

## ii

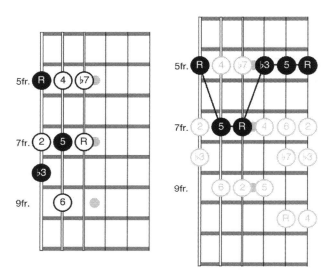

When stacking the 1st, 3rd, and 5th notes from the 2nd position (the Dorian mode) in a way that's practical to play, we get a common Em barre chord shape. Built from the 2nd note of G major, this gives us an Am chord.

Note: As opposed to the 1st mode of the major scale, here we have a flat 3rd. This indicates the note is a half step closer to the root note. You can hear that this flattened 3rd is what gives the chord its *minor* tonality.

Applying this same method to the next position (the Phrygian mode), we see the third chord of a major scale is another minor chord. Built from the 3rd degree in the key of G, this gives us a Bm chord:

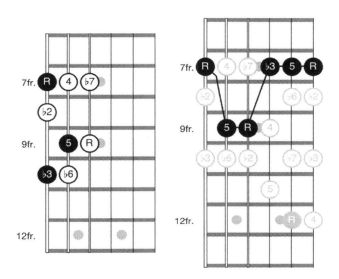

Below we see that the basic triad constructed from the fourth note of a major scale is another major chord. Using notes from the 4th position (the Lydian mode) in the key of G major, we get a C chord:

## IV

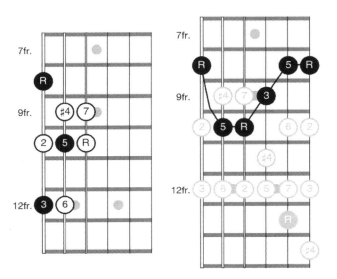

Next, we see that the fifth chord constructed from the 5th position of the major scale (the Mixolydian mode) is another major triad. In this case, a D chord:

## V

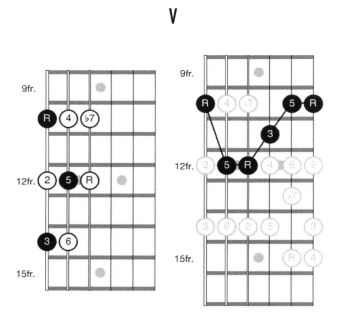

From the 6th position of a major scale (the Aeolian mode), we can stack intervals to build a minor chord. Based on the 6th degree of G major, this would be an Em chord:

## vi

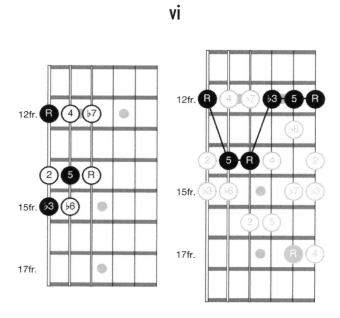

Lastly, through stacking intervals from the 7<sup>th</sup> position (the Locrian mode), we construct a diminished chord. From the 7<sup>th</sup> degree of G major, this gives us an F#dim chord:

## vii°

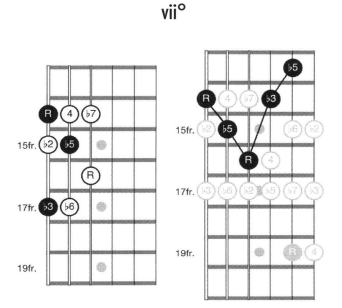

Note: Like a minor chord, a diminished triad is built using a flat 3<sup>rd</sup>. Unlike a minor chord, however, a diminished chord also includes a flattened 5<sup>th</sup>, giving its unique *dissonant* sound.

# Numbering Chords

There's a tremendous amount of information contained within the seven notes of a major scale. Not only can we construct seven different positions from this scale, but these positions also give us seven different chords corresponding to each degree. While there are various chords here, they all use notes from the same major scale. This explains how we can recognize the key of a song by the chords being used. It also demonstrates how we can build chord progressions of our own in different keys.

It's common to attribute numbers to each chord of the major scale in the same way we'd number each scale degree. As demonstrated in this chapter, we often see chords referenced using Roman numerals relative to each chord position. Typically, uppercase numerals represent major chords, while lowercase numerals symbolize minor chords. Diminished chords are often denoted with an additional symbol (e.g., vii°).

Subsequently, a I - IV - V progression in the key of G major would refer to chords built from the 1st, 4th, and 5th positions of the G major scale. This means our progression would be G - C - D.

*Tip: Can a chord belong to more than one key center? Absolutely! As demonstrated, major scales include three major chords and three minor chords. Therefore, it makes sense that any major or minor chord must belong to three different major scales. C, for example, is the I chord of C major, the IV chord of G major, and the V chord of F major. As your playing advances, it's very beneficial to know how the chords in one key relate to other key centers.*

# Extending Chords

At this point it would be appropriate to briefly reference the topic of chord *embellishments*. So far, we've created basic chord forms by stacking the 1st, 3rd, and 5th intervals from each position (or mode) of the major scale. We've also established that notes stacked too close together often sound tense or dissonant. However, this doesn't mean these other notes are never used. On the contrary, additional notes are commonly used in chords *because* of their harmonic complexity.

In fact, placing closely related notes in separate octaves can dramatically enhance the sophistication or richness of a chord. A common example is when a 7th is used to embellish a basic triad. If we continued stacking scale tones to include this interval, our original G chord would become a Gmaj7 chord. Even though the 7th and root are only a half step apart, they sound quite harmonious when played in different octaves:

I

The important thing, if our intention is to stay diatonic (within one key center), is that chord extensions must correspond to their respective scale positions. For example, as already established, like the I chord, the V chord of a major scale is also a major chord. However, their sevenths would be different, because the scale built off of the 5th degree is different from the scale built off of the 1st degree. In other words, looking at both positions, we see that the Mixolydian mode has a flattened 7th, whereas the Ionian mode does not. Therefore, this flat 7th (built from the 5th degree of G major) would turn our D chord into a D7. The difference being that this is a *dominant* chord, as opposed to a major seventh chord:

## V

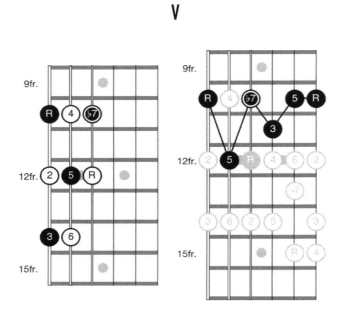

*Tip: Experiment with playing each chord from the same root note. Notice how a seemingly small shift in the structure of a chord can dramatically alter the chord's tonal character.*

# Using Chords

Now that we've established how to build chords using the modal framework, we can explore how this information relates to playing situations. Defining the chords belonging to a particular major scale provides a starting point from which we can create progressions for improvisation and songwriting. As we've covered, each degree of a major scale can be used to build not only a different scale position, but also a different chord. Before creating some progressions to work with, let's review the basic chords in G major. For simplicity, this time we'll voice each shape around the open position.

## Exercise 5.1

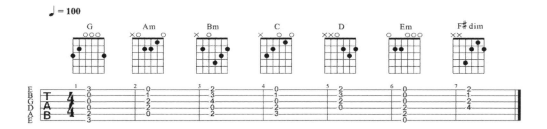

*Tip: Although the chords themselves change between keys, the chord formulas do not. For example, the I, IV, and V chords of a major scale will always be major, while the ii, iii, and vi chords will always be minor. Understanding this makes it relatively easy to transcribe chord progressions between different keys.*

# Tonal Gravity

Having highlighted the basic chords we have to work with, what's next? At this point it makes sense to briefly introduce a concept we'll call *tonal gravity*. This affects our approach to constructing both rhythm and lead ideas. The basic notion is that both chords and melodic ideas have an inherent way of telling us where they want to go. It's like a sense of gravity pulling us one way or another. For example, play a major scale, but this time leave it hanging on the 7th without resolving to the root.

## Exercise 5.2

This just doesn't feel right, does it? The whole scale is pulling toward the root note. It feels incomplete left hanging without resolution. Chord progressions function in a similar way, often needing to resolve themselves by moving back to home base, which is the root (or *tonic*) chord.

> *Tip:* As another example, try playing a diminished chord by itself. Again, you'll notice it doesn't feel stable; it's just crying out for resolution!

This concept reflects the important dynamic of *tension* and *release* as central to any creative vocabulary. Being attentive to where a progression or melodic phrase is gravitating toward gives context to our musical ideas. This works both ways, of course. Intentionally *not* taking something where you might expect can be equally as powerful as taking a progression or melody where it feels it needs to go.

# Building Progressions

Thus far, we've established the basic chords available in the key we're working with. We then isolated some popular chord shapes to use. Now let's look at an example of a progression that demonstrates these chords together.

## Exercise 5.3

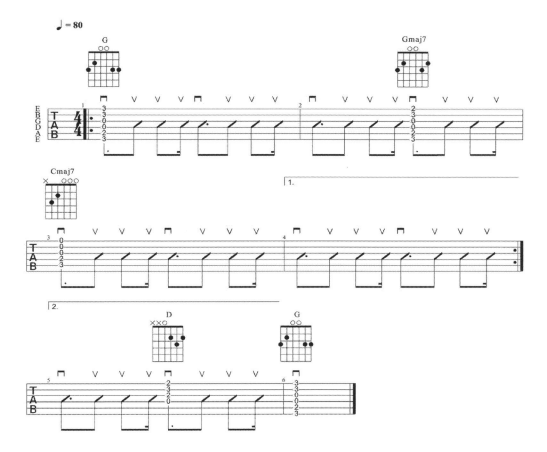

What do we notice about this progression?

- Looking at these chords, we see that the progression uses the I, IV, and V chords of G major. This G major tonality is reinforced by the progression's constant pull back to the G chord.

- The first part of this progression moves between the I and IV chords (G and C). These chords have been embellished with their respective sevenths, adding more color to the progression.

- The last part of this progression moves to the V chord (D) as a turnaround, leading us nicely back to home base at the G chord.

Note: While there aren't strict *rules* for structuring progressions, you'll often see V chords function in this way (leading to the I chord). This is especially true when they're played as dominant seventh chords.

This example prompts the next logical question: Do progressions always have to resolve to the I chord in a major key? The short answer is *no*. Building a progression around the tonic chord of a major key will emphasize the major tonality of the progression. However, this may not always be our intention. For example, let's look at another chord progression.

# Exercise 5.4

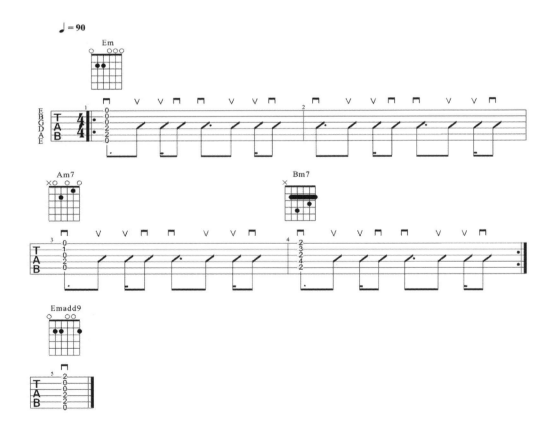

What do we notice about this progression?

- First, the chords being used are the ii, iii, and vi chords of G major. Interestingly, though, there's actually no G major chord here at all! Instead, the progression gravitates towards the Em chord, completely changing the tonal character of this progression.

- Again, there are a few chord embellishments. This progression uses minor seventh extensions for the ii and iii chords (Am7 and Bm7) and also adds a $9^{th}$ to the final chord for interest. This indicates that chords are often extended past their sevenths (by stacking scale intervals, as illustrated earlier).

- Finally, even though this progression sounds distinctly minor, we're still only using chords from G major. As such, our major scale framework is still relevant, despite this being a minor progression!

From these examples, another question arises: Do chord progressions have to stay diatonic? Not at all! Listen to a few jazz standards and you'll hear how easily progressions can move through different key centers. Even in more mainstream music, it's common for progressions to temporarily *borrow* chords from another key or modulate to a different key center entirely. As you progress beyond this book, one important function of modes will be their usefulness in navigating through key changes. While popular music is often based around a single key center, there's no reason your progressions (or even your improvising) have to stay diatonic. The only real defining factor is, does it sound good to you?

> *Tip: Knowing how chords relate to key centers, we can apply this method in reverse to work out how keys relate to chord progressions. For example (assuming a progression is diatonic), any two minor chords separated by a whole step must be the ii and iii chords of the key, because this is the only position where minor chords occur back to back. This is true for major chords as well. The only time they're next to each other in sequence is as the IV and V chords of a key. All we need to do is count back to find our key center.*

# Just a Minor Detour

Before moving forward, let's back up a little bit. We've just built a chord progression in the key of Em using the G major scale. How does that work? The answer, as hinted at, is that each major key also has a minor key that it directly relates to. You may have heard this concept referred to as the *relative* minor. In **Chapter 2**, we explained that the mode built from the 6th degree of a major scale is known as the *natural minor* scale. While the notes in both scales are the same, the sound changes depending on the notes being emphasized (another good example of tonal gravity).

In other words, by learning the G major scale framework we've also (without necessarily knowing it) learned the E minor scale framework. Therefore, we don't need to learn the minor scale and all of its positions, because we already know it! This information relates to any major or minor key center. The patterns are all the same; we're just shifting our starting point to different places on the fretboard.

How would we find the patterns in A minor, for example? Well, knowing that A minor is built from the 6th degree, it's easy to find the parent major scale! If we simply count up two positions, we'll find the major scale we're playing relative to. In this case, the scale shapes for A minor are the same as C major. This would also be true for D minor as it relates to F major, C# minor as it relates to E major, F# minor as it relates to A major, and so on.

# Focus Points

- Closely revisit the information in this chapter. Become familiar with the way chords are built from positions of the major scale by stacking intervals. Experiment with applying this method to construct chords in alternate keys of your choosing.

- Using the chords in G major, try to work out several ways of playing each chord on the fretboard. Additionally, challenge yourself to work out the $7^{th}$ extensions for each chord in the scale. (Again, through the process of stacking intervals from each scale position.)

- Try creating a few progressions of your own using the chords in G major. Don't be afraid to embellish chords with extended sevenths where desired. See if you can transpose your progressions (and the two provided) into different keys. Experiment with playing over these progressions as an introduction to navigating the fretboard in various key centers. Remember, the notes and positions will change, but the shapes will not.

6

# Hidden Chords & Scales

*In this chapter, we'll explore some important concepts for structuring melodic ideas and working with the patterns and techniques we've learned.*

# Introduction

Thus far, this book has been structured step-by-step to help you develop a comprehensive map for fretboard navigation and improvisation. Beyond this, we've touched on various related techniques and key theoretical aspects. The intention has been to provide the appropriate tools for understanding and experimenting with this information.

The bulk of this content has focused on developing a practical command of the fretboard in our approach to lead playing. At this point, it's important to discuss some key ideas invaluable for working with this information in real-life musical contexts. As stated at the beginning of this book, the focus isn't solely on what we play, but also our *approach* to what we play. The most immediate breakthroughs in our playing often come from adjustments to how we *think* as guitar players. In this chapter, we'll explore essential concepts for cultivating musicality within our melodic ideas.

# Strong Notes

It seems appropriate at this juncture to revisit the concept of tonal gravity. If you attempted to improvise over the progressions in the previous chapter, you'll have noticed something quite interesting. Although the notes on the fretboard stayed the same, they sounded different when the tonal context changed. In the first example, the progression pulled toward the sound of G major. In the second example, the progression pulled toward the sound of E minor. This is a fundamental point when thinking about melodic phrasing. Not all notes are created equal in terms of their *tonal* weight. Some notes create tension against the chords they're played over, pulling us one way or another, while other notes feel stable, strong, and resolved. We need both.

Logically, if the chords feel like they're pulling toward a tonal center, it makes sense that the notes played over those chords would feel the same. Typically, we'll find that tones contained within our tonic chord are the stronger notes, because they emphasize the momentum of the progression. This doesn't mean we should only play notes found in a G chord over a G major progression. It simply suggests that these tones typically establish a stronger sense of tonal gravity within the larger scale framework. A popular application of this idea is where a melodic phrase begins on and/or resolves to a note of the tonic chord.

## Example 6.1

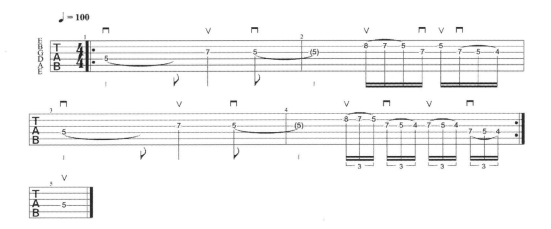

# Hidden Chord Shapes

A practical way to visualize the concept of strong notes is to highlight the basic chord shapes found within each position of the major scale. In the example below, we've isolated the G major chord tones (G, B, and D) within the larger framework. These chord tones are derived from stacking intervals, as discussed in **Chapter 5**. A good analogy when creating melodic ideas is to view these notes as central *branches*, providing stability and structure. In turn, the other notes can be thought of as *leaves*, adding color and interest to the tonal palette:

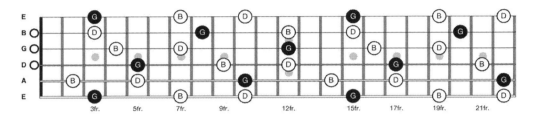

This may seem like a lot of information to memorize. However, looking closer we find that this seemingly random collection of notes actually comprises five basic chord shapes. Most of us are probably very familiar with these shapes, since C, A, G, E, and D are often the first chords guitar players learn:

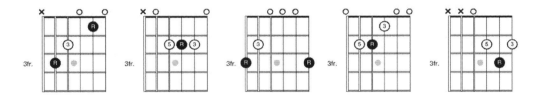

Within the larger framework, these basic chord shapes connect in sequence across the guitar neck. They're built from the G root notes on the bottom three strings throughout the various scale positions.

*Tip:* This concept is often referred to as the CAGED system. Notice that each shape cycles consistently in the C - A - G - E - D sequence moving up the fretboard.

# Major Chord Shapes

Let's take a closer look at these five major chord shapes and how they relate to each position we've been working with. We can see below that every chord shape overlaps one or more major scale position as demonstrated.

## 1st & 7th Positions | E Shape

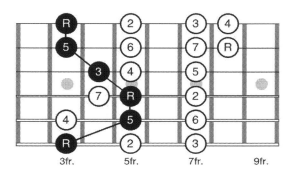

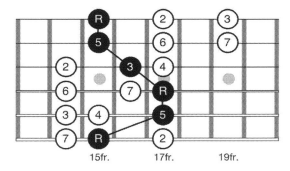

## 2nd Position | D Shape

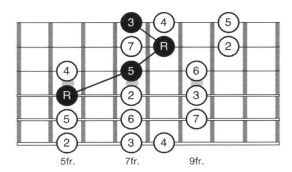

### 3rd Position | C Shape

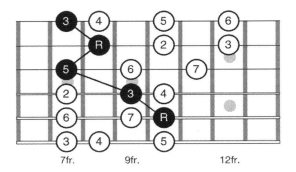

### 4th & 5th Positions | A Shape

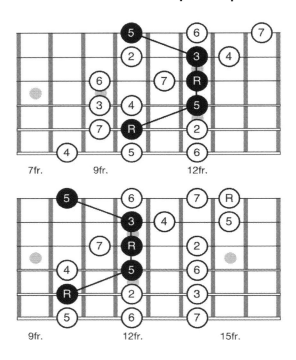

### 6th Position | G Shape

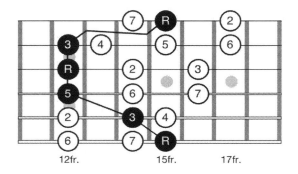

The concept of visualizing chord tones has numerous uses within this framework. For example, we can mirror this same approach with the relative minor scale. Although the overall framework stays the same, we can shift the tonal gravity in the scale to emphasize the sound of E minor. In other words, the chord tones in Em (E, G, and B) now become the *strong* notes we can target in our melodic phrasing. Again, these chord shapes are mapped in sequence across the guitar neck, extending from the E root notes on the bottom three strings:

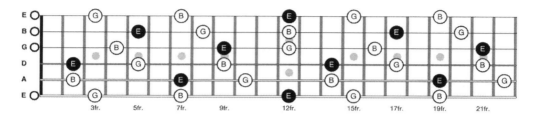

*Tip:* In a minor key, these shapes still follow the C - A - G - E - D sequence. The difference is that each chord is a minor shape instead of a major one. Take note, in either situation both major and minor variations of the same chord shape coincide with the same relative scale position.

# Minor Chord Shapes

The following examples demonstrate the way each minor chord shape relates to the various minor scale positions. Notice that when improvising over a minor progression, the natural minor scale (built from the 6th degree of its parent major scale) now becomes our 1st position, or starting point. Put simply, we're shifting the tonal gravity so that E is now the root note of the scale. In turn, this requires switching the visual reference point within each position (from G to E).

Remember, the framework itself doesn't change; we're only adjusting the notes we want to emphasize. To reiterate, even though the scale patterns shift position, the same basic chord types (in their minor form) overlap the same relative positions of the minor scale.

## 1st & 7th Positions | Em Shape

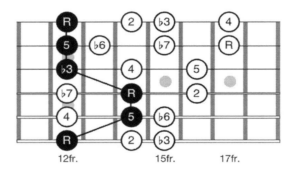

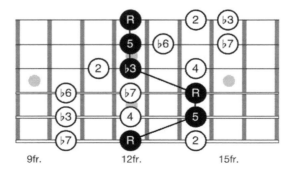

## 2nd Position | Dm Shape

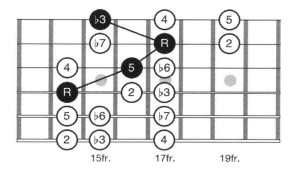

15fr.    17fr.    19fr.

## 3rd Position | Cm Shape

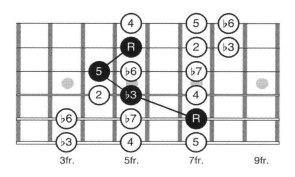

3fr.    5fr.    7fr.    9fr.

## 4th & 5th Positions | Am Shape

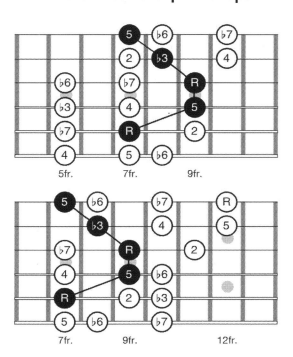

5fr.    7fr.    9fr.

7fr.    9fr.    12fr.

# 6ᵗʰ Position | Gm Shape

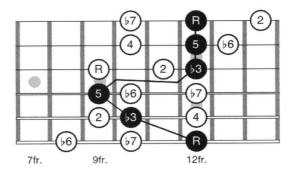

7fr.        9fr.        12fr.

These previous sections demonstrate how to visualize the chord tones, or *strong* notes contained within the larger major/minor scale framework. As we've seen, it's common for a progression to pull toward the major sound of the I chord (major scale) or the minor sound of the vi chord (minor scale). However, we must remember that major scales contain chords from every scale degree. Progressions can also be structured to revolve around other chords in the scale, such as the ii chord or the V chord. This would alter the chord tones we may want to highlight or base our melodic ideas around.

Some guitar players even prefer targeting specific chord tones coinciding with every single chord change in a progression. This is especially handy if a progression moves through various key centers. Often referred to as *playing over the changes*, this approach is extremely common in jazz, among other genres.

*Tip: Don't be overwhelmed by this seeming information overload! The point is that there are various ways to apply the information contained within the major scale and its modes. Put simply, the tonal character of the notes you play will change depending on the progression you're playing over. Just remember to let your ears guide you to the notes and phrases that sound most musically appropriate in any situation.*

# Hidden Pentatonic Shapes

The concept of chord tones having greater tonal weight than other notes is why many use *arpeggios* extensively in guitar playing. (This involves playing, or *sweep picking*, through the notes of a chord in sequence.) Arpeggios are a great way to target specific chord tones in soloing and composition. However, there's another extremely useful way to highlight tonal gravity within the scale framework we've established. This brings us to a discussion of the ever-popular *pentatonic* scale.

Many of us will be familiar with the pentatonic scale. It has become an absolute staple in rock, blues, and country playing. This is one of the first scales we're generally introduced to when we start attempting to solo. What some may not realize is that a pentatonic scale is essentially a major scale, just with a few notes missing. In other words, within the major scale we find the pentatonic scale hiding.

As we know, in a major scale there are four notes separated by just a half step. Melodically, the $4^{th}$ tends to pull down to the $3^{rd}$, and the $7^{th}$ tends to pull up to the root. In a major pentatonic scale, however, these half steps are removed. As such, this tension between notes is avoided, giving the scale a more open sound. Furthermore, without the $4^{th}$ and $7^{th}$, three of the five remaining notes are chord tones (the root, $3^{rd}$, and $5^{th}$):

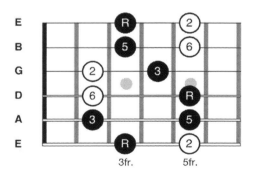

This emphasis on strong notes is even more evident when comparing the E minor scale with the E minor pentatonic scale. Similarly, the minor pentatonic is a five-note scale that omits the half-step movements found in the natural minor scale. Here the remaining notes resemble the exact intervals we find in an Em7 chord (with the exception of the $4^{th}$ degree). Again, three of the five notes in this scale are chord tones from the Em triad. Additionally, we're also left with the flat $7^{th}$, which holds a similar tonal weight because it's such a common minor chord extension:

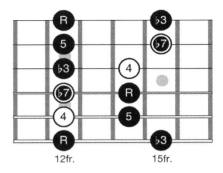

12fr.                    15fr.

Don't worry if this little exercise in theory seems a touch confusing. The main takeaway is that pentatonic scales are full of strong, resolved-sounding notes. That's a big part of why they're so popular; they work extremely well in so many contexts. However, this is also part of the problem we encounter when relying solely on pentatonic scales. We end up limiting the colors available within our tonal palette. Our licks and ideas have a tendency to sound a lot more conventional or predictable given that they're so widely popularized. This isn't necessarily a bad thing, but it can leave some guitarists wanting a little more interest and nuance in their playing. This involves breaking out of these common pentatonic *box* shapes when desired.

# The Hybrid Approach

One main idea being outlined here is that pentatonic scales use notes common to their parent major and minor scales. We've already established that major scale shapes can also be viewed as positions of the natural minor scale. Therefore, logically, both major and minor pentatonic scales are already contained within the larger framework we've established.

Below are the five pentatonic scale positions, one or more of which you'll hopefully find familiar. In the key of G major, we'd consider the initial shape on the left our 1$^{st}$ position. The other shapes can be viewed as inversions of this scale. They contain the same notes but start from different points along the low E string. (A concept you should be accustomed to by now.) It hopefully comes as no surprise that each shape can also be used as positions of the E minor pentatonic scale. In this context, the final shape on the right would be considered our 1$^{st}$ position, because it's built from the E root note:

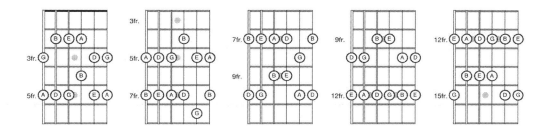

Given their popularity, it's a fair assumption that most guitar players have spent a lot of time playing licks and ideas based around these patterns. Using a modal framework doesn't mean discarding these hours spent. The key concept here is simple: Because these patterns are contained within the larger scale framework, there's no need for an either/or approach. Why not use both? Why not keep using these pentatonic patterns and just embellish them with other colors and tones from the wider major scale framework? Not only is this a more creative way to view pentatonic scales, but it also represents a very musical way to craft our lead ideas.

> *Tip: This approach makes a lot of sense when we understand that pentatonic scales include mostly tonic chord tones. And, as already established, these are generally considered our strongest and most resolved-sounding notes.*

# Major Shapes

As you'll see in the following patterns, we can demonstrate what this *hybrid* scale concept might look like on the fretboard. We're simply picking up the closest notes from the larger framework in direct proximity to each original pentatonic pattern. A more technical way of saying this is that we're adding the 4th and 7th as optional notes to embellish the major pentatonic shapes. And we're adding the 2nd and 6th as optional notes to embellish the minor pentatonic shapes. While they represent different scale degrees, in both the major or minor contexts these patterns are the same.

First, let's look at embellishing each major pentatonic shape with additional notes from the surrounding major scale positions. Notice that the circled intervals represent the chord shapes we've already looked at and how they overlap these patterns.

Note: While the light gray notes are part of each major scale shape, we'll exclude them from these patterns for simplicity.

## Pentatonic Shape 1 | Scale Position 7 | E Shape

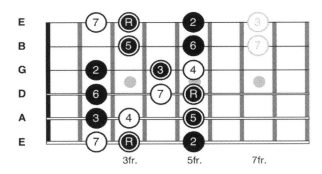

## Pentatonic Shape 2 | Scale Position 1 | D Shape

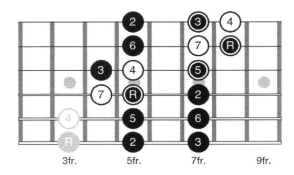

## Pentatonic Shape 3 | Scale Position 3 | C Shape

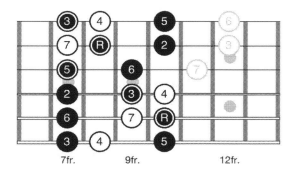

## Pentatonic Shape 4 | Scale Position 4 | A Shape

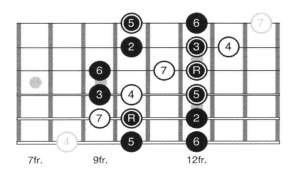

## Pentatonic Shape 5 | Scale Position 6 | G Shape

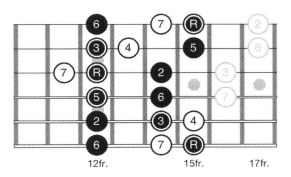

# Minor Shapes

Now let's turn our attention to how the minor pentatonic shapes relate to the wider framework. Again, take note of the chord shape outlined within each pattern. Remember, these patterns are the same as those in the previous section; we're just using the minor scale as our starting point by shifting the root notes.

## Pentatonic Shape 1 | Scale Position 1 | Em Shape

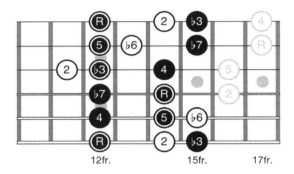

## Pentatonic Shape 2 | Scale Position 2 | Dm Shape

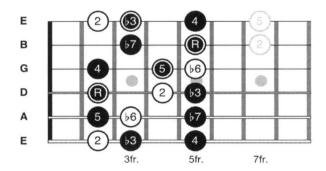

## Pentatonic Shape 3 | Scale Position 3 | Cm Shape

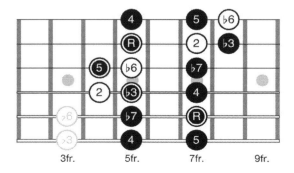

## Pentatonic Shape 4 | Scale Position 5 | Am Shape

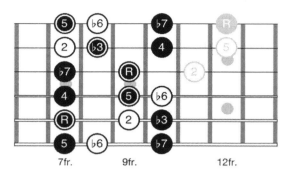

## Pentatonic Shape 5 | Scale Position 6 | Gm Shape

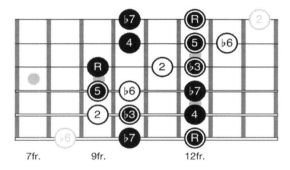

Note: Unlike the previous major patterns, the number alongside each shape and position now refer to minor patterns.

*Tip:* Like the different chords we find within the major scale, there's also more than one pentatonic scale hidden within this framework. We've viewed pentatonic shapes in relation to their parent major and minor scales. This is how they're commonly used. However, we could also build additional pentatonic scales corresponding to other major and minor chords in the key. For example, in the key of G, the IV and ii chords share the same major/minor pentatonic shapes (C and Am). This is also true for the V and iii chords (D and Bm). Admittedly, these additional pentatonic scales won't always give the desired sound, though it's interesting to experiment with them alongside the core shapes we've focused on.

# Visualizing Shapes

As you learn and experiment with each pattern in this chapter, it may be helpful to consider a few final things. There are multiple ways of visualizing these overlapping shapes when improvising or songwriting. Ultimately, this depends on your preferred reference point:

- **Pentatonic Scales:** Perhaps the most popular method is the one outlined in the previous few sections, being mindful of the way chord tones and additional surrounding notes relate to the pentatonic shapes you may already know.

- **Modal Patterns:** Additionally, like the approach of this book, you may prefer to use the modal shapes as your starting point, viewing the various chord shapes and pentatonic patterns as smaller structures contained within this larger framework.

- **CAGED Shapes:** Lastly, you might like to use the five basic CAGED shapes as your key reference point, visually connecting the closest overlapping pentatonic and modal patterns to each individual chord shape on the fretboard.

Essentially, these are just different ways of visualizing the same information. No approach is better than any other, but it's helpful to know which one makes most sense to you. In any case, as repeatedly emphasized, understanding where the root notes overlap in any pattern or position will be extremely useful. Root notes are the common thread between all these approaches.

Finally, if this theoretical exploration into different ways of targeting chord tones and scale shapes has left you overwhelmed, fear not! If you remember nothing else, at the end of the day it's always about using your ears. Developing a theoretical understanding of how things work undoubtedly aids creativity, but it's never a substitute for it. Always favor what you think sounds best over what you assume is more *theoretically* correct. The more you experiment with different ideas, the clearer things become. After all, you can't talk about playing guitar without using the word *play*.

# Focus Points

- Practice moving through the positions of the major scale and focus on the chord shapes found within each position, as outlined in this chapter. Do this in both major and minor keys and experiment with how targeting these notes might influence your melodic ideas.

- Experiment using pentatonic scales within the larger framework. Practice playing the five pentatonic shapes using notes from the parent major/minor scale positions to embellish each pattern. Remember, these *hybrid* shapes are the same in both major and minor keys. Practice visualizing how the modes, pentatonic scales, and CAGED shapes overlap and interconnect with one another.

- Listen closely to a collection of songs you find particularly memorable or emotive (preferably from artists in different genres). Reflect on the concepts covered in the last few chapters. Think about tonal gravity and the way melodic phrases interact with the movement of chords. Consider the note choice, use of melody, and phrasing. What specific things do you notice? What elements make these melodic ideas sound engaging? In light of the ideas discussed, how might you apply these concepts to your own playing?

7

# Motion & Emotion

*This final chapter looks at important exercises for practicing and consolidating the various concepts and techniques we've covered.*

# Introduction

By now we've worked on getting our entire fretboard framework thoroughly in place. We explored the way this *blueprint* can shift to function in any key, not only for improvisation or composition, but also for building chords and understanding chord progressions. We talked about the concept of tonal gravity and highlighted different ways to view the information contained within this larger framework.

In this final section, we depart from the theoretical exploration of the last couple of chapters. We'll turn our attention back to the task of experimenting with this information on the guitar neck. This chapter revisits many of the concepts and techniques we've covered by introducing two fundamental exercises. These exercises are extremely effective for putting things into perspective on the fretboard.

# Melodic Motion

For this first exercise, let's take the G major chord progression from **Chapter 5** and apply some improvised melodic movement over the top. Note that our key focus is on *motion*. While dynamics and expression are a huge part of crafting melodic ideas, these aren't the goal of this exercise. Here are the guidelines we'll be working with:

- This exercise is all about melodic movement; we're *not* trying to solo.

- Listening to the backing track, start slowly with quarter notes (one note per beat) and begin moving around the fretboard in the key of G. Try to do this without stopping or skipping a beat.

- Try not to stay in one place for too long. The goal is to keep moving, covering as much fretboard real estate as possible.

- While maintaining a quarter-note rhythm, try to mix 'n' match among various exercises covered in this book (e.g., moving through two-octave shapes, into single-string patterns, into one-octave shapes, into double-string patterns, into diagonal shapes, etc.). Think about alternating techniques and sequences, switching between alternate picking, legato, economy picking, string skipping, and so on.

- As you move around the fretboard in a consistent and steady fashion, think about the concept of tonal gravity. Pay attention to notes that feel resolved and those that add tension. Experiment with outlining the different chord tones and pentatonic patterns you can see. Challenge yourself to play separately through each modal position, followed by the relative pentatonic shape and then the overlapping chord tones.

- Once you feel fluent with this, try increasing the speed of the exercise using $8^{th}$ notes (two notes per beat). Additionally, you can move to triplets (three notes per beat) and then $16^{th}$ notes (four notes per beat) as it seems appropriate.

Note: Want more jam tracks? Be sure to check out **5-Minute Guitar Jams** as a supplementary practice guide. This book features an album of high-quality backing tracks to accompany your practice.

# Melodic Emotion

The last exercise in motion is fantastic for creatively and intuitively honing our skills at fretboard navigation. However, the end goal is always about taking what we've learned and doing something musical with it. Concentrated meandering around the fretboard (as illustrated in the previous exercise) is a great practice technique, but it should never be our approach for constructing solos or melodic phrases.

For this exercise, let's use the second chord progression in **Chapter 5** and take an alternate approach to playing over it. If the first exercise was about consistent movement, covering as much space as possible, this next exercise is about exactly the opposite. Now we want to limit ourselves by focusing solely on *feel* and *dynamics*. These are the guidelines for this exercise:

- Listening to the backing track, try forgetting all the exercises we've practiced up to now. Concentrate on a single position on the fretboard, preferably staying within one octave.

- It's important to begin this exercise with only two or three notes. Sometimes limiting what we play forces us to be more creative with how we play. Use your ears and experiment with creating simple melodic phrases or *hooks*. Try hearing the melody you want to play in your head before playing it on the fretboard.

- Avoid unnecessarily noodling around on the fretboard. This is an exercise in self-imposed moderation.

- Focus on dynamics, feel, and expression. Practice targeting strong notes. Think about phrasing, use of rhythm, and space. Sometimes what you *don't* play says just as much as what you do. You only have a few notes to use, so don't waste them!

- Draw on every tool you can think of to make these notes work for you. Try experimenting with popular playing techniques like bends, slides, or vibrato. See if you can create something interesting, memorable, and emotive against the backing track.

- Repeat this exercise in multiple positions on the guitar neck. Slowly extend to incorporate more notes as it seems appropriate, but remember, the focus is on feel and melody. Consciously using fewer notes forces us to think creatively about how our melodic phrases are delivered.

*Tip:* *The goal of fretboard navigation isn't to show off what we know by shredding aimlessly all over the place (despite how fast we can do this!). It's so we're empowered to communicate something musical and engaging. A good starting point for crafting solos lies somewhere between these last two exercises, focusing on melodic and interesting ideas while having the freedom to move fluently through different scale positions.*

# Focus Points

- Become familiar with both exercises in **Melodic Motion** and **Melodic Emotion**. These are fantastic practice techniques to revisit regularly, regardless of your skill level. Try switching things around, using the E minor progression to practice fretboard navigation and the G major progression to improvise with short melodic phrases.

- As you work on improvisation (using these or other progressions), be mindful of the chord tones and pentatonic shapes relating to the progressions you're playing over. Practice viewing these shapes as connected to the larger framework we've established. Continue experimenting with how targeting these shapes can influence the sound of your musical phrases and ideas.

- Reflecting on tonal gravity, think about how phrasing, dynamics, and sense of space might complement the notes you play. Experiment using this information to your advantage in creating phrases that sound musical and melodic. Focus on crafting ideas that are interesting and memorable, letting your ears (not your fingers) guide you.

# Final Thoughts

Congratulations on completing *Lead Guitar Breakthrough*!

Unlike other content you might find on lead guitar, the intention of this book hasn't been to bombard you with an arsenal of guitar licks. Nor has it been to offer instruction on the best way to play and sound like somebody else. Although these teaching strategies have their place, our focus was on establishing an overarching framework for approaching any style or genre. The goal was to provide the tools for a comprehensive, well-rounded approach to fretboard navigation. We discussed central concepts in improvisation and songwriting and explored key techniques for experimenting with these ideas.

It's my sincere hope that this book has answered many questions and in doing so has raised many more. This book was never intended to do the thinking for you, but to inspire you to think for yourself. As such, when you refer to this resource from time to time, you may just learn something different, understand something better, or see something you missed previously. This isn't because the content has transformed but because, as your learning progresses, *you* are transforming.

One might expect that the more advanced a person's playing becomes, the less they value the fundamentals. In my experience, however, it has been precisely the opposite. The more you learn, the more you understand the importance of the essentials. This resource has sought to provide a solid, practical foundation for overcoming the roadblocks people encounter in their lead playing. Like all good foundations, this content exists to be built on. It's in the process of moving beyond the fundamentals that we discover just how truly valuable they are.

May this book help inspire you toward continued learning and creativity.

# Liked This Book?

Did you find this book useful? You can make a big difference in helping us spread the word!

While it would be nice to have the promotional muscle of a major publishing house, independent authors rely heavily on the loyalty of their audience. Online reviews are one of the most powerful tools we have for getting attention and finding new readers.

If you found this book helpful, please consider helping us by leaving a review at your place of purchase. Reviews needn't be long or in-depth; a star rating with a short comment is perfect. If you could take a minute to leave your feedback, it would be sincerely appreciated!

# Additional Resources

For more resources, including great free content, be sure to visit us at:

**www.guitariq.com**

Stay in touch with all the latest news. To connect with us online, head to:

**www.guitariq.com/connect**

Would you like to read more? For a complete list of Luke's books, check out:

**www.guitariq.com/books**

Remember to grab your online bonus! Get the free bonus content for this book at:

**www.guitariq.com/lgb-bonus**

Interested in a master class with Luke? To check out his online workshops, go to:

**www.guitariq.com/academy**

# About the Author

Having played for over 25 years, Luke Zecchin is an accomplished guitarist with a wealth of studio and live experience. Outside his work teaching music, Luke has toured extensively alongside renowned national and international acts, performing at everything from clubs, theaters, and festivals to various appearances on commercial radio and national television.

Playing lead guitar, Luke has worked on projects with established international producers and engineers. He has been fortunate to see these collaborations break into both the Top 50 ARIA Album and Singles charts, having also received nationwide airplay and notable debuts on the Australian iTunes Rock charts.

As the founder of **GuitarIQ.com**, Luke is dedicated to the education and coaching of guitar players all over the globe. With books available in over 100 countries worldwide, he has emerged as an international chart-topping author in his field.

Luke continues to work as an author and musician from his project studio based in the Adelaide Hills, South Australia.

Find him online at **LukeZecchin.com**.

Printed in Great Britain
by Amazon